7/21 | | | Anfic

TROEON
TURNINGS

TROEON
TURNINGS

CYRIL JONES
PHILIP GROSS
VALERIE COFFIN PRICE

Troeon : Turnings

Troi, aredig, cerdded, treigl dŵr...

Yn y gyfrol Troeon : Turnings mae dau fardd sydd â'u gwreiddiau mewn gwahanol draddodiadau yn cyfarfod yn y cytir rhwng cyfieithu a chydweithio. Daw Cyril Jones o gefndir disgyblaeth y gynghanedd a Philip Gross o gefndir mwy amrywiol ac aflonydd barddoniaeth Saesneg. Yn hytrach na gresynu nad yw'n bosib atgynhyrchu clymau ffurf a chynnwys ieithoedd trwy gyfieithu, maen nhw yn ymddiried yn ei gilydd i ryddhau egni o'r newydd ar sail y gred fod haearn yn hogi haearn.

Ar waetha'r storm a'r hwthwm o glefyd,
geilw haf ei fwrlwm
adar i dewi'r larwm
a churo'n galon trwy'i gwm.

Yn yr un ysbryd mae Valerie Coffin Price yn chwarae'i rhan hithau trwy gyfrwng dyluniadau trawiadol ei hargraffwaith, gan roi tro annisgwyl i iaith y ddau fardd a chreu ymwybyddiaeth newydd o'i phosibliadau.

Cyril Jones is a Welsh language poet who writes strict and free metre poems. Since moving to work in south Wales in 2001 he has collaborated with artists, an archaeologist, and other poets.

Mae Cyril Jones yn ysgrifennu yn Gymraeg trwy gyfrwng y mesurau caeth a rhydd. Ers symud i dde Cymru yn 2001 cydweithiodd ag arlunwyr archaeolegydd a beirdd eraill.

Mae Valerie Coffin Price yn arlunydd/llythrennydd sy'n ymateb yn greadigol i farddoniaeth a lleoedd. Mae'n siarad Cymraeg, a ddysgodd fel ail iaith, ac mae hyn yn ei galluogi i ddarganfod y gofod rhwng y beirdd a'r ieithoedd.

Turnings : Troeon

To turn, to dig, to plough, to upset, to translate… Bend, lap, journey, time...

The Welsh word troeon unfolds meaning after meaning. In Troeon : Turnings, two poets confident in their own traditions meet in the hinterland between translation and collaboration – Cyril Jones from the disciplines of Welsh cynghanedd, Philip Gross from the restless variety of English verse. Rather than lamenting the impossibility of reproducing any language's unique knots of form and content in translation, they trust each other to explore the energies released.

> In the cloud chamber, atoms tear, spin, split,
> translate the past and future
> into spirals, spun silk, sheer
> release, the heart of the matter.

In the same spirit, Valerie Coffin Price plays an equal part with striking letterpress designs that surprise the language of both writers into new awareness of its possibilities.

Philip Gross is a poet, librettist and writer for young people. A keen collaborator with other poets and across art forms, he has lived and worked in South Wales since 2004.

Mae Philip Gross yn fardd, libretydd ac yn ysgrifennu ar gyfer pobl ifanc. Bu'n byw yn ne Cymru ers 2004 ac mae'n gydweithredwr brwd â beirdd eraill ac ar draws gwahanol ffurfiau celfyddydol.

Valerie Coffin Price is an artist-letterer, whose work responds creatively to the poetry and place. Being a second language Welsh speaker enables her to explore the space between the poets and the languages.

Seren is the book imprint of
Poetry Wales Press Ltd.
Suite 6, 4 Derwen Road, Bridgend, Wales, CF31 1LH
www.serenbooks.com
facebook.com/SerenBooks
twitter@SerenBooks

The right of Valerie Coffin Price, Philip Gross and Cyril Jones to be
identified as the author of this work has been asserted in accordance
with the Copyright, Designs and Patents Act, 1988.

ISBN: 978-1-78172-606-8
ebook: 978-1-78172-607-5

A CIP record for this title is available from the British Library.

The publisher acknowledges the financial assistance of the Books Council of Wales.

Printed by Pulsioprint, France.

Contents

FY NHRO I YW FY NHRYWYDD

A FY HER,

DY BRO DI FYDD

NESA - A THRO I'R MEYSYDD

And here, between one rib of bedrock and the next, the river takes a turn
which may be a shift of the light, or the season,
                                        or of register, of tone,
the way the same words eddy on
                                your voice or mine,
                                                into or out of tune,
from chapel hymn to a patter of sunlight, sounding brass to a rattling tin,

the part-song passing (we are only ever part) from tongue to tongue.
The water ironed to a sheet, tucked down,
                                        rucks, is tangling, is torn
in a slalom of stone
                        or darkens, dwelling on
                                        a memory, the pristine
source: in a slate light, the switch of the wind on the back of the tarn,

and everything since has been a running. Or it falters, has a *funny turn*
as Grandmother said (but strange, no one
                                was laughing) as if a cartoon
ghost had whispered: *Have a long lie down.*
                                She did, soon.
                                                But we return,
words muttered in the sleep of languages, or rivers, as they toss and turn.

Troeon

Y troi oesol a'r trosi
ddaw'n ôl â'n hafonydd ni
afon Taf fu i ti'n dafod
f'afon Arth hen dduwies fu'n 'wherthin
dan geulan. Hithau dy Fechan nawr yn fwy
yn cywiro hanes ger Mynwent y Crynwyr,
hen fydr ddoe a fu yn fudr, ddu
heddiw'n hau lluniau yn ei llif
rhai yn groyw yn y graean
ond yn gaeth i gytseiniaid hen gân
y lle sydd gywydd o gwm
a'i goed a'i lethrau'n godwm
serth, yn gell o linellau
clo fel yr hafn sy'n culhau
o'r pen 'rholl ffordd lawr i'r pant
a'r lli'n corddi lle cwrddant...

yn welyau o alawon
am ennyd yn cydblethu cynganeddu yn wir
ar asennau craig rhesi ohonynt
yn dudalen fel hon rhwng deiliach
a'u gofer yn troi'n gymer o gerdd
dy alaw di a chyfalaw fy eilio
yn rhyw gerdd dafod od o gerdd dant
dau hanner ar y cyd yn dihuno'r co
rhyngom ac yn slalom dros gerrig slic
neu'n cael eu smwddio'n gynfas
o ddŵr bas (neu ddwfn) rhyw bwll
cyn i awel ddechrau cyniwair
awel dro yn bwl (annisgwyl) drwg
mamgu'ma gynt *cerwch i orwedd*
meddem ac fe aeth – gorwedd
mewn hedd am hir
ond yma o hyd mae hwyl
ar hynt ar gerrynt y geiriau
a llefarant yn llifeiriol
yng nghwsg maith ieithoedd
neu afonydd fel y mae'r rheini'n
trosi troi
ein cân yn eu cwsg.

Turnings

The perpetual toss and turn
where rivers flow backwards;
the Taff to your tongue,
my river *Arth* the hidden she-bear, goddess
into my memory's bank. Taf Fawr, Taf Fechan,
mirror-clear, meditating on its history
near Quaker's Yard, sowing reflections where it
meanders – and then a wobble between pebbles

My *Arth* will always be captured
in the echo of its consonants

Its seven-syllables of a cwm
a headlong of slopes, a heirloom,
steeped in a past that narrows
to a cell, a funnel where it flows
from head to heart, to sing
hymns (no dancing!) but turning

from one rib of bedrock to the next
        to a duet of riverbeds
      where a breeze lifting, leafing
       accompanies the confluence of this song
         the melody and counter-melody
           a strange combination of *Cerdd Dafod, Cerdd Dant*
         two halves awakening common memories
           like a lullaby, once a slalom over its slippery stones,
         or the ironed sheet of the shallows
           before a hidden baton beckons
          an unexpected cross-breeze
           when we told grandmother *Have a lie down*,
          and she did – for long, and in peace...
          but here the *hwyl*
            is a forever flowing current of words
            in the dream of languages

                or rivers
                      as they toss and turn
                      our songs in their sleep.

Moor PG

Is it a time of my life,
      the times we're in, is it simply
          a time of the night

makes *rivers flow backwards?*
      Not that I believe
          there's a spot or a drop of our headwaters

that can get us pure and true
      any more than the damage downstream
          which makes us. I've been listening to you

dissolve yourself back into *Arth*,
      that one long syllable that's equally
          growl from the cave of the past, and earth

finding voice (itself, it seldom
      speaks) in water... and now this is me
          not asleep or awake, at 3 a.m.

      and I'm Dartmoor – not *back on* or *in*
but *am* (if this is a dream
      I am the moor's dream, not it mine) –

a dim mass, till I start to name
     its waters, brook by leat
by stream by river: Meavy, Plym

         and Walkham, Erme and Yealm
     and yes, an Avon and a Tavy:
dark seeps, brightening, out of the dumb

heart of peat, on their separate ways
     into articulation, north, south, east,
west, towards opposite coasts, and whose

         language is whose, I don't know.
     Release them. But I could believe
I have it – have us – for a moment, whole

         in our scattering. So far to go

till we regather, in the lingua franca of the sea.

dwylo'r dŵr

dŵr rhaeadr

fy heniaith lithrig

rhyd fwdlyd

y blaenau'n y niwl

afoniaith Dwyfor

afonydd a'u henwau

dwfrfyfyrio

for every drop that falls, a choice:
drain or river, river or drain?

the kingfisher's reflection
splintered off and flew the other way

going grey in the rain –
dim-eyed river in puddle-glass specs

hey molecule,
which river were you last time down?

they say a wan girl
threw herself into a story by this weir

the conscious river, slowed
to perfect reflectivity

it's too late now to reconsider river-hood
it is a one way street

downhill: is that relaxing into gravity?
or bundling it up in armfuls to smuggle away?

river, when I'm gone
will you remember me?

a muddy ford: the beasts come down to drink
from history

the river: a machine for polishing this pebble
and this one and this one and this...

white water: its excitement
trying to be light

oes fer yw oes diferyn:
lawr, lawr i afon neu lyn

glas y dorlan yn nrych dŵr
yn ffoi'n fellten, ffordd arall, i ffwrdd

rôl glaw, llwyd yw ei lli'
prin y gwêl drwy'i sbectol bwdelog

foliciwl chwareus,
ar sawl llithren ddŵr fuest ti?

taflodd merch lwyd, medden nhw,
ei hun i drobwll ei chwedl fan hyn

yr afon o'i gwirfodd a arafodd;
a mwy, mor wych yw drych ei dŵr

rhy hwyr iddi 'styried ei rhawd
unffordd; hynny yw ei hanffawd.

Afon Rhiw: a yw'n ildio i ddisgyrchiant?
neu'n codi'i phac wrth redeg bant?

afon, pan af
a fydd fy nghân yn dy gân, ar gof?

rhyd fwdlyd – lle daw'r bustych
i ddrachtio hen hanes

na, dwylo'r dŵr wela i, yn rhoi sglein
ar garreg gron ac ar hon a hon a...

dŵr rhaeadr a'i gyffro gwyn
 yn trio troi'n oleuni

Bear's Hill

CJ

This time, it's the morning mist, dissolving back
to *mynydd bach*. Mountain? I doubt.
And *bach?* True, but I prefer the other meaning
– endearment. Endeared hills,

with their triad of lakes – *Eiddwen, Fanod, Farch,*
names that sometimes flow,
to be tributaries between languages.
Was it *Farch* into marches, or marches into *Farch?*

Some have the ring of colonists
on the ear – Bear's Hill, smallholding, *lle bach.*
Sounds deceive, looks can lie.
Its inhabitants – a time-warped threesome;
Jane *mam wen*, stepmother come housekeeper,
the father, small-time farmer, *tyddynnwr,*
Jack, the son, teacher-poet,
his lyrics neat, rectangular stanzas, *englynion*
visual reminders of a previous era's
enclosed fields, peat bogs,
when houses mushroomed;
one-night-stands of defiance, *tai unnos,*

against landowners – *y Sais bach.*

(no endearment this time!)

And back to that kitchen table,
placing consonant-laden lines on eisteddfodic scales
to discover that they were lopsided,
or lapsed, post-Georgian lyrics
always a leg – or an arm – short of an eisteddfod chair.
The listening:
literary anecdotes, off by heart quotes –
Waldo, Keats, Parry-Williams, Hardy.
It's taken a lifetime to grasp
that the learning was seldom in the teaching
but in the (yes you're right) in the dissolving
back into languages, in the flight of imagination,

returning like red kites to *Mynydd Bach*,
turning, climbing invisible stairways,
crossing freely above old frontiers
of fields, poetic metre, language, credo,
tilting tails – that are pens in our hands,
with their ambivalent flick of meanings,

tilting like feelings – always forked.

RHWNG TAFODAU IEITHOEDD . .

THINGS

TRIBUTARIES BETWEEN LANGUAGES

TROU

Bear's Hill

CJ

Gallaf innau ymdoddi, dychwelyd eto
i'r ardal – Mynydd Bach. Ond mynydd? Go brin.
Nid bach chwaith,
bryniau, falle, yr ildiwn i'w hanwyldeb

O Frynteirllyn mae Eiddwen a Fanod yn ddrychau
llonydd a llyn Farch yn farf o frwyn,
maen nhw'n llifo'n rhagnentydd i'n tafodau weithiau.
Ai Farch yw *Marches* neu *Marches* yw Farch?

Ond gwladychwr wyt ti *Bear's Hill*
uwchlaw afon Arth,
y tŷ hir, y lle bach a'i drindod
o breswylwyr nad aeth, ar ryw olwg, trwy wddwg
twndish amser i'r ugeinfed ganrif:
Jane yr howscipar, y tad a'i straeon dilyn march,
ac yntau'r bardd-athro o fab:

pob telyneg ac englyn o'i eiddo
yn betryalau ar dudalen i'n hatgoffa
o fynydd a gaewyd yn sgwariau twt gynt
gan wanc mistir tir – y Sais Bach o swydd Lincoln;
pan godai'r preswylwyr, dywarchen wrth dywarchen,
eu protest unnos yn dai.

Dychwelyd i'r nos Suliau
pan osodwn linellau beichiog o gytseiniaid
ar y dafol eisteddfodol, ar fwrdd y gegin,
a darganfod eu bod ar sgiw
yn ymarferion Sioraidd a chwythodd eu plwc,
neu'n goes neu fraich yn fyr o gadair fy ngwobr.

Y gwrando wedyn:
y chwedlau llenyddol, yr adrodd o'r frest –
Waldo, Keats, Parry bach, Hardy.
Deall, am y tro cynta, taw yn y cofio
mae'r dysgu, pan fo ieithoedd
yn codi ar aden

yn dychwelyd fel y barcud i Fynydd bach,
yn cylchu, dringo grisiau anweledig yr aer,
uwchlaw llefydd, gormes, cred a mesurau barddol,
marchogaeth thermalau'r dychymyg
fel y llinellau ar dy dudalennau,

eu cynffonnau'n braidd-symud
fel hen gwilsyn mewn llaw,
ac fel ein cerddi
yn fforchog.

Penny PG
(Plymouth)

The back way, down beneath the station,
was Pennycomequick. It made sense:

where you'd come from the clogged fields,
from thin pickings at the moor edge, here

where the Great Western steamed in, trailing clouds
of glory... out, upcountry, where the world was

probably. Or stop a night, a week, beneath the king's
head on the pub sign, on its golden guinea,

ready for a spin. That's language at its quantum
tricks: both heads and tails, both right and wrong.

Dowse here; follow the culvert, under the suspiciously
flat park to
                    suddenly, a rich mud stink: the creek

that opens into Tamar and the Sound, the sea – that seeps
down from another language: *Pen-y-cwm-gwyk.*

Just up the cwm, the head, the pen... (Yes, don't shun
that pun either. Write it.) So the penny drops.

Glasffrwd   CJ
(Ystrad Fflur/Strata Florida)

Picture headwaters
frayed, on a map, waters that are split hairs,
then flow to become a name, a single stream.
Listen to *glas*,
with its extended vowel, like 'far',
the blue of the sky reflected in the meaning,
in clearings,
and mirrored in other words:
glaswellt, the freshly grown grass
or *glaslanc*, laddish, young and loud.

Then, there's *ffrwd*, the fast flow,
so cool, rhymes with 'dude'.
This fluent stream,
with its wells, – magnets on its banks,
for those upstream pilgrims seeking healing,
those downstream monks for whom they were holy;
for today's poets, gazing into dark waters
for pennies they can't spin for inspiration.

Glasffrwd could be the name for all ages,
all streams,
flowing, forever fresh,
towards the river

Teifi,
the mother tongue.

Glas

Glaslanc
Ffrwd

Glaswellt

Glasffrwd

headwaters on a map

the blue of the sky

laddish, young, loud

the fast flow

this fluent stream

the freshly mown grass

flowing
forever

the name for all ages

ONCE. ONCE UPON A BARE PLOT LIVED A STORY … ONCE THE FALLING RAINDROP HAD THE WHOLE WORLD AT ITS FEET. ONCE, ONCE… (SEE? I CONTRADICT MYSELF ALREADY.) ONCE… (PLEASE TELL ME IF YOU'VE HEARD THIS ONE BEFORE.) ONCE FOLK HAD FINGERS FINE ENOUGH TO PLUCK THE STRINGS. ONCE THERE WERE EAGLES IN THIS POST CODE. ONCE IS AN ONLY CHILD, THE SECRET FRIEND OF NOW. ONCE IS AN ACT OF FAITH; HOW COULD YOU EVER KNOW? ONCE DOES NO ENCORES SIMPLY TAKES ITS BOW. ONCE, NO ONE HAD TO TEACH YOU HOW TO SING. ONCE THE LANGUAGE HAD NO NEED FOR PLURALS. ONCE, OUR GRANDMOTHERS (OR THEIRS BEFORE THEM) HAD WINGS. ONCE COMES ON WIDE-EYED, OH SUCH INNOCENCE. ONCE [A LONG PAUSE] AH, THAT PERFUME… ONCE, AND AGAIN: THAT OLD ROMANCE… ONCE LIVED IN THE HOUSE NEXT DOOR, BUT SHE MOVED. ONCE, IN THE REAR VIEW MIRROR, WITH A SORT OF WAVE, MAYBE TO ME. ONCE IS AN UNLUCKY BIRD; BLOW IT A KISS. ONCE LEAVES A CLEARER FINGERPRINT THAN YEARS OF TOUCH. ONCE BURIED IN THE CELLAR OF AGAIN. LIKE THIS… ONCE IS JUST SO ELOQUENT; IT BEARS REPEATING. DON'T. ONCE WE HAD A HORIZON, NOT JUST AS FAR AS YOU COULD SEE. 'ONCE,' THOUGHT HERACLITUS, DIPPING ONE TOE IN FOREVER. ONCE, WE COULD USE THE WORD 'ONCE' WITHOUT IRONY. ONCE WAS HIS SECOND NAME. TRULY, WHAT WERE HIS PARENTS THINKING? I GET THE FEELING THAT I KNEW YOU ONCE, HE SAID. I WONDER WHY, HIS WIFE REPLIED. ONCE IS A DOOR THAT HAS ALREADY SHUT BEHIND YOU, CLICK. ONCE, NOBODY NEEDED TO SPELL IT OUT, KNOW WHAT I MEAN? ONCE COMES FREE; ALL THE REST YOU HAVE TO PAY FOR. 'ONCE,' THINKS THE RIVER LEAPING DOWN, THE SALMON LEAPING UP. ONCE IS OLD STUCK VINYL JUMPING IN ITS GROOVE. AS HE GREW DRUNKER, EVERY OTHER SENTENCE STARTED 'ONCE…' ONCE TELLS ITS STORY ONCE TOO OFTEN TO BE TRUE. MY GRANDFATHER HAS A RUSTY TIN OF ONCES, LEFT OVER FROM THE WAR. THE RELIEF SHIP NEVER REACHED THE COLONY OF ONCE. ONCE IS THE FAULT LINE, WHERE TECTONIC PLATES OF AFTER MEET BEFORE, HE NEVER EVEN LEARNED HIS ONCE-TIMES TABLE. ONCE BITTEN … MY AUNT NODDED LIKE A KIND OF NO. 'NUFF SAID. HOW TO PROTECT THE PURITY OF ONCE? DON'T LOOK BACK. OR ANYWHERE AT ALL. AT THE END OF ALL EXCURSIONS ONCE IS WAITING LIKE A TERMINUS. ONCE PLAYS A BROKEN HARP STRING, INCOMPARABLY. ONCE OUTSIDE THE GATE, HE SAW THAT LONELY WAS JUST ONE MORE KIND OF HOME. ONCE, WE COULD TALK ABOUT THE FUTURE. FANCY THAT. ONCE, IN THE CORNER OF THE ROOM, SITS WATCHING. WATCHING. ON HIS MONUMENT, HIS NAME, AND ONCE, NO OTHER EPITAPH. ONCE DOESN'T HAVE, OR NEED, OR WANT, MEMORY. ONCE, IN THE LANGUAGE OF UTOPIA, WILL HAVE A FUTURE TENSE. ONCE THERE WAS A RIVER. END OF. IT WILL NEVER REACH THE SEA. ONCE. ONCE. ONCE

Unwaith

Cip deryn ar dderyn oedd e, un bollt
o dan bont o'i nythle
'n eiliad sy'n para'n 'wele'
cefnglas, a'r ias yn hwre.

Quick

Bird-spark or arc-flash, blue shot from the dark
of the bridge, full throttle
from nothing, from 'who?' to '... *wha-a-at?*'
– star of the moment, spotlit!

Unwaith

Cip deryn ar dderyn oedd e, un bollt
o dân bont o'i nythle
'n eiliad sy'n para'n 'wele,'
cofinglas, a'r ias yn hwre.

Nostalgic

Blue flint cracked on black, the stone of the bridge
– my first time – left alone
staring after, the bird flown,
always the one and only.

Aesthetic

A trick of the light, or free play of sun
on the stream – sight's hearsay:
one flash, précis of a day,
free gift, like grace. Or cliché.

Photographic

Click. There, you've caught it, light dead on the page,
the loss of it mended
maybe... like love, a word said
best when it's not expected.

Metaphysic

Think this: bird-flash on its nest in the night,
flight fixed at the quickest,
still: light-speed made manifest,
come home to itself. At rest.

PS. On a Manner of Turning

in the cloud chamber, atoms tear, spin, split,
translate past and future
into spirals, spun silk, sheer
release, the heart of matter

Tracts

The pressure of the word,
the way it's brought to bear
on paper
       :Gutenberg
and all at once they rise
in flocks, riffling wings
of pages:
       the chitter and shriek
of great contentions swirl
into the winds of history.

Those early printer-preachers
clattering out broadsides: turn,
turn, over-
       turn the known
world – tracts as in 'a tract of land'
seen from a high bare hillside
or the ink-shod
       metal impressing
the page like the hundred mile plod
of drovers' roads to market.

Close up and fading, print
by print, each letter's face betrays
its wear
            which is to say
its self – the way a month
of drought brings up the scar
of ditch, field
                  or deserted village.
Ground we've once disturbed does
not forget   as we do.

Even the air my Methodist
great-grandfather hammered with
the Word
            bears traces. Sea mist
rolling up the moor side thins
and shreds so shapes move through
– a darkening
                  of rock or
patient beast or judgement coming,
who knows which or whether close or far?

Troedigaethau CJ

Y geiriau a wasgwyd
ar ddalen cof yn ifanc
i lithro dros wefusau llwyd

ac erchwyn reilin Sêt Fawr-
fel y brefarhyddam yr afonydd...yn rhibyn
lle'r oedd cynulleidfa'r cegau mawr

yn bysgod mud yn eu meimio. Y geiriau
fu'n nofio'n yr awyr yn ddiystyr
am hydoedd. Nofio, ymwáu

y mhowlen ei ben yn gaeth,
cyn dechrau magu adenydd
a chael... ie... rhyw fath, o droedigaeth.

Troi'n adar yn dod nôl â dail eu hystyron
yn eu pigau weithiau.
Nid digon, mae'n wir, i'w troi'n nyth gron

o gred, waeth roedd y nen erbyn hynny
yn gyfeiliant aflafar gitarog
geiriau na fu 'rioed yn gaeth dan glawr du.

Ond am heno digon i'r droedigaeth
ei ffurf ei hun wrth iddi hedeg
yn drindodau drudwns o batrymau iaith

ar draws hon, wybren heno'r dudalen,
cyn clwydo'n freuddwydion pluog
dan reilin bargod dy ben.

YMFUDIAD...

MIGRATIONS

englynion

DIPPER

Bronwen y Dŵr

Pendilio, dalgwympo'n y dyli'n gaib
feddw gorn, cyn iddi
yn llwyr ddiflannu i'r lli'
a'i ias ebrwydd i sobri.

BRONWEN Y DŴR

Dipper

He teeters, sways, about to sprawl face first
in the drink. A pratfall:
splash! He's dunked... just to crawl
out dry, as if teetotal.

THE BLUE HERON

Y Crëyr Glas

Ei lyfr yw ffrydli Hafren a geiriau'i
gerrynt mae'n ei ddarllen:
delwi, heb droi tudalen
yn glust i'w redegog lên.

Y CRËYR GLAS

Heron

The Severn's tongue-flick and flow is his text.
He is his own tableau:
deep reader, rapt, his shallow
page always turning to go.

WILD GEESE

Gwyddau gwyllt

Mae'u cwa-cwa uwch Ionawr y cwm, a'i hin
yn dyner, fel rhigwm
lleddf am ddyfodol llwm
sy'n alarus, yn larwm.

Wild Geese in January

No wistful lyric, their Where-where-do-we-
go? but an afterword
in flight, a weeping, hard-wired
alarm bell, never answered.

GWYDDAU GWYLLT

Wild Geese Warning

New Year, too mild… A rhyme too sure, their where-
where? to be true: over-
head, their one sad word whose pure
rhyme's itself, not the future.

GWENNOL

Gwennol

O law i law â'r wennol hon, ar wib,
drwy'r we, rhwng gwehyddion
heddiw a ddoe ei throeon
dros dir a diaros don.

SWALLOW

Migrations

1

swiftshuttle   thinning weft laid on the warp
of tongues timezones nation
states   dry lake beds   boats gone down
like birds   lost in translation

2

deft as a click, their flights cross-thread the space
between us, weave rooted
with routes, the quick with the dead –
a web, a world enfolded

3

a glance, eye to eye, hand to hand, a glint
on the airwave – returned,
then to now, nowhere to stand
on earth, the sky its homeland

STARLING

Aderyn yr Eira

A single beauty, sheen like sun-sparkle
on snow: is this more than
or less than itself: this one
star sans its constellation?

Starling

O'r cytser fe ddaeth dy seren, yn befr
haul bardd ar dudalen;
dod ar siwrnai'n llatai llên
i'n rhynnu o gell Branwen.

ADERYN YR EIRA

Mulfran: mule-crow:

half-heraldic, mixmatched, mongrel,
a sturdy first cross
of cool-eyed snake and canny corvid

– a bit too much neck
quite to know what to do with at rest –

four or five in a hunch midstream above
their shuddering reflections
on a hummingly

high tension cable,
un-scorched but
as if pre-shrivelled by the shock

of time (think archaeopteryx,
think a fossil in flight)

and what became of us :

the sagging power lines,
large-bore pipes,

whole towns of thirst and wastage
cross-lacing the course of the Taff,
like a body rusting

past retirement age,
all its workings on show.

Say *crooked*
and you've got the mule-crow wrong
:that one straight flight

upstream or down
(just cutting a meander here or there)

is the measure of things,
whatever water does
the true meridian

round which our dry fields
our papery brick plains

warp and flutter,
sheets pegged in the wind.

Blown away. Now

the mulfran unfolds,
is off

up to the far bright water-bodies
of the sheep-despoiled uplands
or down to the high tide

held in
we would like to think forever

by the bonny
trumped-up buttress
of the Bay.

TROEON

TURNINGS

I thought his reflection in the river's flow
was nothing but the same again
reversed... until I turned
to face it. Tried
to read his lips. Leaned
closer, face against a window pane
which shattered. So, now: which of us is who?

TURNINGS

TROEON

Fall

The way it seems to idle to an almost-
pause
       before the flip-
           top drop
at the lip of the weir

then sleeks over, combed and glossed...
How it shrink-
       wraps each ridge
              of the rippling
slope. And then trips

into buckling, a regular frizz... The way
it rips
       and tangles, dis-
           composed
gone to froth thick

as milk, patience come to the boil,
a seething
       under/over
           thrashing upstream
like a change of heart

– it was all a mistake, this running
away to sea – or
       like something recalled
           when it's beyond
recall but oh... The way

it turns through every permutation
of itself
       within itself
          moto perpetuo
or perfect verse form or

the coolest way on earth to boil, to burn...

Eddy

The way that recoiling re-
                        cursive we twist-
turn to catch at our own tales
                        our myths,
of the Fall, to mend it
                        with our running stitch
of question marks...
                        The way we flinch
from every granite nudge
                        of shoulders
in the crowd, as if
                        it were the boulders
in a hurry, not the stream,
                        the press
of landforms leaning too close,
                        to confess
what's been eating
                        away at them, drip
drip, at their strata,
                        at their sleep...
How we repent, re-
                        pine, yet reel on
still glancing back,
                        how we yearn.
Not for us
                        the clear whoosh
of the mill race
                        or the channelled sluice
but like my mother's
                        fond-intricate
way with unravelling
                        jumpers to knit
ourselves into ourselves,
                        weave what
was into is, what might
                        be into what is not.

Meet

The way our maps are stitched
                              with them: *Two*
                              Waters, Watersmeet...
We're drawn to them, to bridge,
to build, to drive a wheel.
                              Never clearer to me
                              than the sepia, fresh
from the peat, from the mist
mires, the pickling of
                    Iron Age bones,
                    of Meavy into Plym's
milksop murk, runoff

from rich decay of granite
                         into china clay,
                         all shades of
cornflower blue to white
in ranks of settling pools,
                         by ruined pyramids
                         of waste. The way
they inter-tumbled miles

downstream... How there are *abers*
                              far inland as if
                              to say when one
of water's tongues meets another
a mouth speaks, like fever
                         to chill, dark to light,
                         acid to alkali. Let's taste
the difference together
without merging into bland,
                         no dilution, one
                         curling round
the other, turn-taking and

returning. The way I'm listening now.

UNWAITH YW'R ENNYD, A HONNO'N YMSON Y PEDWAR AMSER. UNWAITH YW'N CÂ
HEB AFIAITH EN-CÔR. BU UNWAITH YN UNIAITH - WIR. UNWAITH YN DDRWS STOR
SAWL STORI. UN TRO HEFYD WNA'R TRIC. IE, TRO. UNWAITH FEL ELENI, WE
HWN, HEN DRO CAS AR HEWL HANES. UNWAITH YN DDYN, UNWAITH. YN DDYN
OND DWYWAITH, MEDDAI HI. ANTI, YN BLENTYN. SAWL GWAITH Y'I CLYWAIS, S
Y GWEUD: UNWAITH ROEDD HENWR. AETH HWNNW'N ORMES UNWAITH YN ORMO
MAE GAN MAM-GU LOND CÔL, LOND CAE O 'UNWEITHIAU' OD AR DAFOD EI DWEUD
UNWAITH ROEDD HWCH A AETH AR RWYDD HYNT, EBE HI, YN LLAWN BYWYD. YN
PLOP, CWYMPODD I'R PLWMP... IE, HEN DWLL, YW PLWMP, UN DWFN. HEN DR
WIR, OND NID HEN DRIC. UNWAITH - HER I AMSER YW. HEB DDOE, HEB ECHDOE,
BYTH. UNWAITH HEB FORY NA THRENNYDD. GALL UNWAITH FOD YN FAITH NEU
FYR. GALL FOD YN DDI-RIF, YN GANRIF, NEU JYST YN 'GYNT'. IE, IE, GYNT — FEL
GWYNTOEDD; Y RHEINI A CHWALODD YR US AR UNWAITH. NEU'N UNWAITH SY
RHYW NOS SADWRN, YN SIWRNE. BETH, YDI UNWAITH YN GALLU MYND AR DAIT
DWED?' SÎWR IAWN, WIR, DIAWCH, MAE SIWRNE'R DAITH AC UNWAITH YR UN PE
YN SIR GÂR. UNWAITH YN LLE A SIWRNE, YN BOB SUT. YN DAITH AC YN SEFY
YN STOND. UNWAITH O DRAS NEIS, ROEDD 'NA ENETH DRWS NESA. YN GUSAN Y
ÔL I'R WAL AGOSA. YN GARIAD AETH ALLAN O GYRRAEDD. YR UNWAITH A AETH
HIRAETH OEDD HWN. NEU'R MELYS GUSAN SY'N FAB (NEU FERCH) SY'N FYW O H
ROEDD HWNNW'N GUSAN GWAHANOL! YN UNWAITH A ALL DROI, NEU A AETH,
GENEDLAETHAU. UNWAITH EIN HAP, UNWAITH EIN HWYL —AC, IE, EIN HER. DA
SÊR, BU DAWN SIARAD HEN FAM-IAITH UNWAITH AMSER MAITH CYN FY MOD. N
UNWAITH SY'N HENO, YN ATEB UNWAITH ETO DY EIRIAU, DY LINELLAU FAN H
YR UNWAITH A DRODD YN DDWYWAITH YN DDWY IAITH SY'N CYD-DEITHIO.
ANADLU YN HUAWDL AR DUDALENNAU EIN HAWEN. Y DDWY HYN A FU UNWAI
SAWL GWAITH YN MYND I'R GAD BENBEN, OND FAN HYN AR UNBONT. EU HANGER
YN CYDGERDDED, A'U DAU LAIS YN CYDOGLAIS RHWNG DEUGLAWR, YN RHWT
DDIBROTEST. EIN HUNWAITH SY'N RHYW FATH O GYNGHANEDD, YN ATSAIN DIW
CYTSEINIAID DEUAWD. IE, DEUWCH, DARLLENWCH, A RHOWCH IDDYNT EICH LL
AM UNWAITH, TRWY YMARFER AMYNEDD. RHOWCH GYNNIG YN FFONETIG AR
IAITH Y NEFOEDD. A NOFIWCH, BRACSWCH UNWAITH YN BRAF AR EICH HYNT TR
GERRYNT Y GEIRIAU — Y RHAI DIERTH Y TU HWNT I'R DEALL. HEDDIW AR FÔR Y GE
DORFA O EIRIAU, MENTRWCH, DA CHWI, AR GWCH Y GERDD. UNWAITH YW EI E

Y Delyn Dros Daf   CJ

Telyn ddur
yw'r bont dros Daf
ond â'ch traed mae'i chanu;
sbonc ei halaw yn wefr dan wadn.
Traw pob cam yn codi'n
uwch cyn cyrraedd ei chanol,
lle mae'r sefyll fel bod yn sedd y duwiau,
                                    gorsedd amser.
Dros y ganllaw ucha
mae'r llif bron yn ddisymud
a'i düwch fel cysgod llwch y cwm
a fu'n dagfa ar degwch am ganrif a mwy.

Ond ein tynged bob gafael
yw syllu ar lif pob ddoe
a sŵn rhaeadr fory'n byddaru ein clyw.
Ac wrth syllu dros y ganllaw isa,
anodd dweud pu'n ai chwerthin neu sgyrnygu
mae'r ewyn.

Harp/Telyn :
footnotes for a lost translation

[1]   A bridge that is suspended, strung from itself to itself in
tension without which it would crumple, a dumb tangle,
                                                    is a harp
that anyone can play by touch, by foot soles, without knowing,
here in mid-air, mid-stream, where we also hang,

[2]   Maybe the wind, by night, is feeling for the fingering;
the rain, tuning itself drop by drop, by microtones;
                                                the river,
hustling its not-quite-regular vibrations into almost soundwaves
we can feel in the footsoles, or the soul.

[3]   Harmonics, resonance… That sounds like accord. But why
do you think a marching platoon must break step
                                           or the answering
thud and spring becomes a spasm, whiplash, chord-clash, self-
crescendo that would tear itself to bits?

[4]   Rather, consider how the patient angler stood in midstream,
in his still bow-wave and eddy, casts
                                   a near-transparent long
slow wave-form down the filament to where the fly will kiss
the surface, barely leave a trace.

[5]   To grasp for the import of *telyn*, glossary in hand, to tease
out the literal strands of it, note by footnote by note
                                              is to lose
the fluid tautness that connects/translates it, past to future. Or
maybe it's just too close to touch.

[6]   In ballads of a cold North shore, the dead girl's wave-white
breastbone is washed up. He gives it strings,
                                       the itinerant harper,
all unknowing – and is struck dumb as anyone when that night,
in front of all the people, it begins to sing.

[7]   Listen…

Telyn

equals plucking honeyed notes,
caressing tender strings you don't play but 'sing' in Welsh;

sing to the accompaniment
of a consensus of consonants;

to the tune of the hymn's golden instrument,
the pilgrims' eternal trek home;

that equals the shape of Arthur's constellation
in the northern hemisphere's skies;

strings that are couplets of lines
you adjust with the ear's keys,

according to the room's humidity,
the hearth's symphony of crickets.

Now it's the lounge corner odd-shaped heart,
that sometimes-symbol of high art,

so different to its yesteryear's little sister's
triad of strings – with Nansi's infectious fingers'

sparking hob-nailed beats on the pub's stone floor.

Telyn
now robed, shrouded, ready to be
clumsily manouvered – and cursed – by theatre hands,

through the open hatch-back
of the Volvo-in-waiting.

*Note: Nansi Richards was a well-known Welsh harpist from mid-Wales.
She played the 'delyn deires' – the old Welsh harp with 3 rows of strings.*

| Chwedl y Tair Afon | A Fable of Three Rivers | CJ |

Yn llifo – gorlifo
pob un â'i thir a'i thon
ei hunan.

flowing – overflowing
each one weaving its own wave
its own breeze

Ias,
ger Clas-ar-Ŵy,
wrth lithro i'r dwfn
i gerrynt mas o'i gyrraedd e
y gwyliwr ar y geulan.

The Wye
near Glasbury
where she delved the deep
on a current beyond his reach –
the witness on the bank.

Afon Wysg
a gwres Gorffennaf wedi'i dadwisgo
i droelli yn un ffrwd siapus
a'i gwely llydan o raean
rhyngddi a'r geulan
mor anniben.

River Usk
stripped by July's heat
to meander sleepish and shapely
with its wide gravel bed
so dishevelled between bank
and channel

'Dere,' meddai,
wrth gamu i anwadalwch cwch
yn harbwr Bryste,
'ac fe ddangosa i ti'r lle
a roiodd i fi fy llais
newydd.'

'Come', she said,
stepping on board the wobbly boat
in the harbour,
'and I'll show you the place
that gave me
my new voice.'

Roedd bad ei fyfyrion e'n croesi
gorwel dwy ganrif
i fwrdd y *Maria*,
a'r criw o Gymry a bresgangiwyd –
gan amser y tro hwn. Fe'u cludwyd
fel c'lomennod a'u tynghedu
i ddychwelyd fesul pluen
yn eu llythyron 'sha thre.

His meditations' boat
crossed two centuries of horizons
to the deck of the Maria
where a Welsh crew remain
pressganged – by time now. Then ferried
like pigeons and fated to return
feather by feather in their
homing letters.

A thu draw i'r drofa,
lle mae *Avon* a phob afon yn uno

And beyond the bend,
is the mouth where the Avon and every
afon become
gravity and time defying words

i drechu disgyrchiant ac amser

that flow back over mountains and millennia

trwy ddringo mynyddoedd a millennia

to babble the lingua franca of rivers –

gan uno i glebran lingua franca afonydd –

afoniaith na all ond ceisio
angori yn y galon

a tongue that can only attempt to
anchor in the heart

69

New Voice

A new voice downstairs
      in the old house
where we've lived for years,
      voice half familiar,
half strange in its trickle and ebb –
         first quick then...

a catch in the breath
      as if with a shudder
and creak like spring
      melt on the frozen stream
a crack was opening,
        an ice-locked half a century

of empire fissured, crumbling,
      where the old-now-new
small states are stepping apart,
      still numb and slightly
breathless –
        people stepping through...

like the Estonian uncle we've
          been waiting for and who
this must be on the doorstep now
          and he is...
but speechless still
                    as I come down to see

that it's my father speaking – his,
          the new-old voice no one in this
half-life of his has heard,
          that stands now
with snow on its boots, dark water
                    lapping in the space between

us here in the carpeted hall
          of a semi-detached in Plymouth
too suddenly small
          to hold us – who we are, and
were, and who we might (who I might
                    never) have been.

... lies still

dark,

a cavern acoustic

perfect reflectivity

anything you say

about a river,

in whatever language,

is translation.

dwfrfyfyrio

the river: a bystander
always pointing 'they went thataway'

the weir: a dream of cutting water
with a concrete blade

headwaters in the mist where moor and cloud
are one thing, they begin

Tamar, Severn, Usk, Wye: these rivers
they rise within sight of the sea
and head the other way

the short steep Dwyfor, growing guttural
in flood, rolling its boulders to the sea

a city without a river seems unfinished
or unstarted, only provisionally there

river: a long established habit
water can't unlearn or forget

give me a river for my birthday
so I can take it with me wherever I go
(or do I mean vice versa?)

towns change, even mountains; names
of rivers are deeply etched
(there are *afons* everywhere)

where *water/wasser/vatten* splashes
dŵr lies still, dark, a cavern acoustic
(there is more to this than sound)

anything you say about a river, in whatever
language, is translation (imagine its voice
before the first voice, the first ear)

rwyt ti bob amser yno
yn dweud 'fe aethon nhw ffordd 'co'

yng nghored fy heniaith lithrig
mae'r geiriau'n chware mig

y blaenau'n y niwl lle mae'r rhos
a'r cwmwl yn un a lle tardd

Tamar, Hafren, Wysg a Gwy: codant
o fewn golwg y môr
cyn rhuthro i'r cyfeiriad arall

wrth rowlio'i cherrig mawr tua'r môr,
gyddfol, yw afoniaith Dwyfor

hebddi, mae dinas fel petai'n
anghyflawn, heb fod, neu dros dro, bron

hen, hen arfer yw afon,
'haws cofio na dysgu,' medd hon

ac os ca i afon yn anrheg
gallaf fynd â hi i bobman
(neu ai hi sy'n fy nghludo i?)

trefi a mynyddoedd, gallant newid,
ond afonydd a'u henwau, sy'n ddwfn
fel eu gwlâu (aberant ym mhobman)

lle mae nant, afonig, ffrwd yn ffraeth
mae pyllau dŵr yn ogofa'n acwstig
(eu hystyr sy'n ddyfnach na sain).

dwed ym mha iaith a fynnot
am afon, mae'n gyfieithiad (dychmyga
lais ei llais cynta, ac ust y glust gynta)

PRIN

print closes

a spatter of shadows
dries to blotches.

windscreen fogging

the wings of the word
folded,
           fading,
macular.

1.

Racks of the word
hung up like sides of meat,

fish drying in the smokehouse.

The wings of the word
folded.
There's a time

for keeping and a time to fly.

2.

Print opens. Every ink mark is a pane.

(Do you remember Playschool? *What's through
the round / the square / the W-*

shaped window?) There's rain

like a spatter of shadows dissolved
that dries to blotches. Memory:

the thing itself

concealed as much as carried by its residue.

3.

The frame, the clamp, the rack.
The instruments of pressing
out in ink
           what words confess

4.

… or like the clack-and-
clunking apparatus
with its levers, straps and stops

the old church organist climbs into
pump-and-cranking till
with a shuddering wheeze

we are wrapped

in one big voice that blunders
into praise – voice
of the hammer-beam and buttress

and the emptiness between,

a voice we rise to, voice you could believe
the endless vowel, the deep
guttural, of God.

5.

Print closes
with its fading,
macular.

The last impression is a windscreen fogging
or, who knows,

another vision ripening:
that of a tired and blemished
face that watches us

until we fall asleep.
Its care.

Tributary

Track it back to the source and here
you have... what?
                    This singular
seep out of bog moss, among many.
Here: that fondest story, that
        of *born-to-be*

which is always told backwards.
Land surveyors
                have announced the One
at whose feet others lay their tributes
to his Name, like petty kings
        on an Assyrian frieze,

as if every trickle down the hillside,
every dribble
                from my eaves,
was not equally the river. As if every
last unasked-for whisper in the corner
        of the eye or mind,

every niggle or whim disowned was not
by equal title
                    me.

HELIGAN
HELYGEN

a renga in *englynion milwr*

TRAIL

TRYWYDD

Fy nhro i yw fy nhrywydd
a fy her, dy dro di fydd
nesa – a thro i'r meysydd.

AR GOLL

Scrub willow… *helygen:* I'm
on your trail, *trywydd*, through rhyme-
gardens lost to sand, to time.

Tir ar goll, mae'i gât ar gau;
ar stryd, Treverbyn, gair strae
yn eco rhwng y craciau.

LOST

ECO

Who owns an echo? The quick
of Kernow is seamed in rock
cracked, fire-warped, metamorphic.

GWYTHI

SEAMED

O wyll oer gwythiennau llaith
eu cwyn fu'n eco unwaith;
mae'n rhwydd ar y mwynwyr iaith.

GROANS

TOMENNI

The groans of bedrock – pain or
warning? Wheal Fortune, Geevor
gone... Spoil-heaps of metaphor.

.

HEART

Mae llwythi tomenni mud
Dylife'n edliw hefyd:
calon blwm ddoe bwrlwm byd.

CALON

The heart of the cracked geode,
not void: *vug*, quartz-bristled word
in Kernewek. Silent. Heard.

GWACLE

VOID

O wagle pwll yn hyglyw,
hen air sy'n ddiferyn yw –
a fu'n ddylif, yn ddilyw.

POOL

PWLL

Mute pool: among the bone white
clay hills' waste its more-than-sky-
blue stare meets God's, eye to eye.

GWEN

WHITE

A daw'r haul yno i droi rhod
'dalen wen a chreu pennod
ei oleuni yn löynnod.

TROI

Each breaker's foam redraws land's
end – new breath, old words returned
heard. Held. Healed. Passed hand to hand.

...0

[Ewyn pob ton yn ail-ddarlunio'r
pentir. Hen eiriau'n tynnu ana'l eto'n
y clyw; rhai triw o'u trin, o law i law.]

LAW | LAW
HAND TO HAND

YN ECO RHWNG Y CRACIAU

Treiglo   CJ

camu o iaith i iaith – treiglo
yn ddibasport, ddibwrpas
trwy glwyd lle mae tir ar glo

from stanza stone to stanza- to and fro
to these lines time and land-locked
the eye, voice and ear trio

dros bont heb dalu toll
er bod y dreth ar amynedd yn para
yn nhir y geiriau coll

to the bridge with no tolls to pay
but beyond its chains
the tax on patience remains

gwibio o lôn i lôn
yn y frawddeg-gerbydau ddiatalnod
siwrne yw sy'n siâr o'i nod

where we muster grace
sentenced to the unpunctuated queue
of the vehicles' snail pace

drwy'r pentre nad yw – a fu – unwaith
cael rhedeg yn reddfol wrth roi llais
i'r meddal trwynol a'r llaes

to the place where the mutations' kissing gate
swings on the ear's hinge
soft, nasal and aspirate

hap yw pob cyrraedd
ond yn swyn y trioedd hyn dros dro
mae tir pobl ac iaith yn rhoi gwaedd

destination is always pure chance
and in these lines' triads
land, language and tongues throng once   eto

more

treiglo, to travel, mutate

94

Mutations

the way proximity
    one sound before the next
becomes a bridge

suspends the ear's disbelief

like persistence of vision
    how the shuffling of moments
in the Arrivals hall of eye and brain

become a journey

or wayfaring photons bent
    by the mass of black hole neutron star
arrive with news

of what's unseen between

the way at last sound softens
    warmed by body heat
the human contact

no word that is truly heard remains unchanged